BASEBALL

BASEBALL: BATTING

BRYANT LLOYD

The Rourke Press, Inc.
Vero Beach, Florida 32964

PHOTO CREDITS:
All photos © Lynn M. Stone except cover © Chris Luneski

EDITORIAL SERVICES:
Penworthy Learning Systems

Library of Congress Cataloging-in-Publication Data

Lloyd, Bryant, 1942-
    Baseball, batting / Bryant Lloyd.
      p. cm. — (Baseball)
    Includes index
    Summary: Describes how to grip the bat and hit the ball, stances and swings, the hitting zone, bunting, base hits, making outs, and more.
    ISBN 1-57103-184-7
    1. Batting (Baseball)—Juvenile literature. [1. Batting (Baseball)
2. Baseball.]
I. Title II. Series: Lloyd, Bryant, 1942- Baseball.
GV869.L56 1997
796.357'26—dc21   97–17505
                                                                        CIP
                                                                        AC

Printed in the USA

TABLE OF CONTENTS

THE HITTER

A hitter, or batter, is the baseball player who bats against the other team's pitcher. The hitter uses a long, rounded bat made of wood or metal. The batter tries to hit the pitched ball with the bat.

The hitter's job is to reach base or help a base runner get to another base. The batter usually does the job best by getting a **base hit** (BAYS HIT), such as a single, double, triple, or home run. A hitter can also reach base by **walking** (WAWK ing) or being hit by a pitch.

Colorful language is part of baseball. A hard-hit ball that travels through the air in a more or less straight line is sometimes called a "rope."

The batter's left foot steps forward into the pitch, and his right foot turns in a squishing motion as he begins his swing in a Little League game.

THE BATTER'S GRIP

The batter grips the bat with both hands around the bat handle. For a right-handed hitter, the left hand grips the bottom of the bat handle and rests on or near the knob of the handle. The right hand grips above and against the left hand.

A left-handed batter, hands together to grip the bat, eyes the next pitch.

A batter's grip allows the wrists to turn as the swing follows through. The wrist movement is called "breaking your wrists."

If a player **bunts** (BUNTS), or taps the ball, the grip changes. A batter who wants to bunt does not swing the bat. (See page 17)

THE BATTER'S STANCE

A batter's stance is the way a hitter stands while waiting for a pitch at home plate.

Usually, a batter's feet are toward the plate, spread about one and one-half times the width of the batter's shoulders. As a batter's feet are spread more or less apart, the stance is said to be more "open" or "closed."

The batter's knees should be bent and the batter should lean slightly toward the plate. The shoulders stay even with the ground.

This batter, knees bent, bat cocked, feet even with the plate, has a fairly open stance.

THE SWING

Hitting a baseball takes great timing between hand and eyes, or eye-hand **coordination** (ko AWR din AY shun). A batter's hands should be about shoulder height for the swing. A right-handed batter's hands should be about even with the right armpit.

A batter's head turns to watch the pitcher, then the flight of the pitched ball. A hitter should watch a pitch reach the bat.

The swing should be level, at the same height as the pitch. The batter's arms unbend with a swing.

A batter who hits a sacrifice fly or makes a sacrifice bunt, which moves a base runner ahead one base, is not charged with an official time at bat.

A smooth, even swing should be level with a pitch. Sometimes hitters chop at a ball or undercut it.

MEETING THE BALL

A right-handed batter steps into the pitch with a six-inch (15 centimeter) stride of the left foot. The right foot stays on the ground but turns, or pivots, with the swing. The right foot acts like it's squishing a bug.

The batter's swing greets a pitch and sends it up. In the foreground, a pitcher's right leg kicks up during the follow-through of the pitch.

This left-handed batter finishes a swing with the bat still gripped in both hands over his right shoulder. Some batting coaches teach a one-handed follow-through.

The swing brings the bat through the ball, driving it with force. The batter finishes the swing facing the pitcher and the bat, still gripped, over the left shoulder.

THE HITTING ZONE

The area in which a hitter likes a pitch is that hitter's zone. Some hitters, for example, prefer pitches toward the outside of the plate.

Every hitter, however, must learn to hit any pitch within the entire **strike zone** (STRYK ZONE). The strike zone is the area over the plate and from the hitter's shoulders to the knees. If a hitter doesn't swing at a pitch in the strike zone, the **umpire** (UM pyr) will call a strike.

A sacrifice fly is a fly ball that is caught but that permits a runner to score from third base. To score after a catch made with fewer than two outs, the runner at third base must not leave the base until the catch has been made. Then the runner may race for home plate.

This pitch was delivered in the batter's strike zone, just below his shoulders. The batter kept his eyes on the ball, swung smoothly, and hit it.

BUNTING

A bunt is an attempt by a batter to hit a pitch just a few feet past the plate.

For a **sacrifice** (SAK ruh FYS) bunt, a hitter squares around toward the pitcher. A right-handed hitter slides the right hand about 16 inches (41 centimeters) up the bat handle, keeping the left hand at the knob.

The batter holds the bat across the plate, as if it were a target. The bunter then simply tries to raise or lower the bat to meet the pitch.

A hitter ready to bunt squares in the batter's box to face the pitcher. A bunter must be prepared to pull back the bat if the pitch is out of the strike zone.

MAKING OUTS

Hitting a baseball is not enough to reach base safely. In fact, far more often than not, even good hitters make outs!

If a batter hits a fly ball that is caught, the batter is out. If a batter hits a ground ball that a fielder throws to first base before the batter reaches it, that batter is out.

The difference between being safe and out may be a half-step. This batter is digging for first base even before the ball is out of the picture!

18

A third baseman fires the ball to first base. If his throw beats the runner to the bag, the runner is out.

Three strikes also make an out.

To reach first base, or beyond, a batter usually needs to hit a ground ball past the infield—or hit a ball past the outfielders.

BASE HITS

A batter who reaches base safely may be rewarded with a base hit. To earn a hit, the batter must not have caused another runner to be out. There must also have been no fielding **error** (ER uhr) on the hit ball.

A one-base hit is a single. A two-base hit is a double. A three-base hit is a triple. A fly ball hit in fair territory beyond the playing field is a home run.

The number of official times at bat helps determine a player's batting average. Walks, like sacrifices, are not added to the total of official times at bat. To figure a batting average, divide the total of base hits a player has by the times at bat. For a major leaguer, three hits in each 10 at bats (.300 batting average) is excellent.

This ball, hit past the shortstop, was a one-base hit, or single.

GLOSSARY

base hit (BAYS HIT) — a single, double, triple, or home run

bunt (BUNT) — to tap a pitched ball just a few feet into fair territory

coordination (ko AWR din AY shun) — the result of groups of muscles working together in smooth motion

error (ER uhr) — a fielding mistake, such as a dropped fly ball, that allows a runner to reach base

sacrifice (SAK ruh FYS) — a ball hit in such a way that it causes the batter to be out, but advances a base runner

strike zone (STRYK ZONE) — the area over the plate and between the batter's shoulders and knees

umpire (UM pyr) — an official on the field who makes decisions about the game, such as fair or foul, ball or strike

walking (WAWK ing) — going to first base after the pitcher throws four balls

Little League coach helps a young batter with his stance at the plate.

110683

INDEX